T0030987

# Tree Frogs
## Life in the Leaves

By Moira Rose Donohue

Children's Press®
An Imprint of Scholastic Inc.

Content Consultant
Pete Johantgen
Headkeeper, Shores
Columbus Zoo and Aquarium

With special thanks to
Joseph R. Mendelson III, Ph.D.
Director of Research, Zoo Atlanta

Library of Congress Cataloging-in-Publication Data
Names: Donohue, Moira Rose, author.
Title: Tree frogs: life in the leaves/by Moira Rose Donohue.
Description: New York, NY: Children's Press, an imprint of Scholastic Inc., 2020. | Series: Nature's children | Includes index.
Identifiers: LCCN 2019004832| ISBN 9780531229934 (library binding) | ISBN 9780531239155 (paperback)
Subjects: LCSH: Hylidae—Juvenile literature.
Classification: LCC QL668.E24 D66 2020 | DDC 597.8/78—dc23

Design by Anna Tunick Tabachnik

Creative Direction: Judith E. Christ for Scholastic

Produced by Spooky Cheetah Press

Printed in Heshan, China 62

SCHOLASTIC, CHILDREN'S PRESS, NATURE'S CHILDREN™, and associated logos
are trademarks and/or registered trademarks of Scholastic Inc.

1 2 3 4 5 6 7 8 9 10 R 29 28 27 26 25 24 23 22 21 20

Scholastic Inc., 557 Broadway, New York, NY 10012.

Photographs ©: cover: Nicolas Reusens/Getty Images; 1: David Liittschwager/National Geographic Creative; 4 map: Jim McMahon/Mapman®; 4 leaf silo and throughout: stockgraphicdesigns.com; 5 girl silo: NadzeyaShanchuk/Shutterstock; 5 frog silo: ilikestudio/Shutterstock; 5 bottom: Thomas Vinke/imageBROKER/Getty Images; 6 frog icon and throughout: Koshevnyk/Shutterstock; 7: ARCO/P. Wegner/age fotostock; 8-9: Joe Riis/National Geographic Image Collection/Alamy Images; 11: CathyKeifer/iStockphoto; 12 center: Design Pics/Getty Images; 12 bottom: Dirk Drotlef/The Royal Society; 14-15: Sean Crane/Minden Pictures; 17: Jelger Herder/Minden Pictures; 18-19: Buddy Mays/Getty Images; 20-21: J.M. Storey; 23: George Grall/Getty Images; 24-25: Roy Toft/National Geographic Creative; 26-27: Kike Calvo/Getty Images; 28-29: Dan Suzio/Science Source; 31: John Sibbick/Science Source; 32 top left: Quentin Martinez/Biosphoto/Getty Images; 32 top right: simplydave/iStockphoto; 32 bottom left: Dennis Donohue/Dreamstime; 32 bottom right: Pete Oxford/NPL/Minden Pictures; 34-35: Paul Hobson/FLPA/Minden Pictures; 37: JasonOndreicka/iStockphoto; 38-39: Brian Gratwicke/Flickr; 40-41: Melba/age fotostock; 42 left: Arun Roisri/Getty Images; 42 center: gary powell/Shutterstock; 42 right: Mark Bowler/Science Source; 43 top: Ch'ien Lee/Minden Pictures; 43 left: AnnaBreit/iStockphoto; 43 right: Takeda Shinichi/Minden Pictures; 43 bottom: B. Trapp/Blickwinkel/age fotostock; 46: Design Pics/Getty Images.

# Table of Contents

# Fact File: Tree Frogs

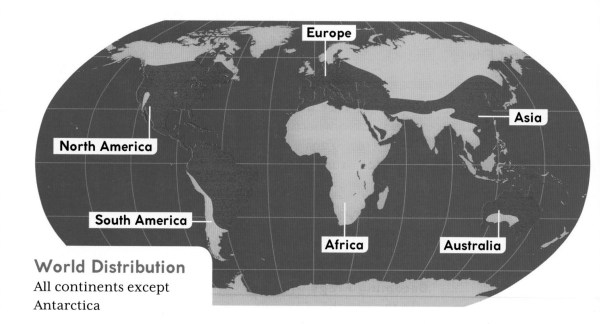

Europe

Asia

North America

South America

Africa

Australia

## World Distribution
All continents except Antarctica

## Habitat
Trees near water in forests and wetlands; some species can live in cold or dry climates

## Habits
Hunt at night; sleep during the day, camouflaged or otherwise hidden from predators

## Diet
Insects and worms, swallowed whole and alive

## Distinctive Features
Slimy skin, long legs and toes, and sticky toe pads

**Fast Fact**
Tree frog predators include snakes, bats, owls, and other birds.

## Average Size

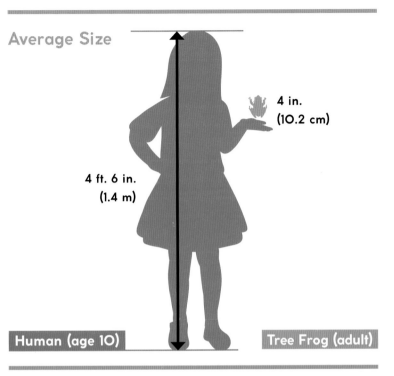

4 ft. 6 in.
(1.4 m)

4 in.
(10.2 cm)

Human (age 10)    Tree Frog (adult)

## Classification

**CLASS**
Amphibia
(amphibians)

**ORDER**
Anura
(frogs and toads)

**FAMILY**
Hylidae
(tree frogs)

**GENUS**
More than 47 genera

**SPECIES**
More than 700 species,
including:
- *Agalychnis callidryas*
  (red-eyed tree frog)
- *Hyla versicolor*
  (gray tree frog)
- *Hyla cinerea*
  (green tree frog)
- *Phyllomedusa sauvagii*
  (waxy monkey)

◀ **This is a waxy monkey tree frog. Its skin is coated with a waxy substance.**

5

CHAPTER 1

# Living the Tree Life

High in the rain forest trees, a tiny red-eyed tree frog snoozes with its legs tucked under its green body. It's hard to see where the leaf ends and the frog begins. *Tht-tht-tht . . .* The frog hears a sound close by. Is it a snake? Suddenly the frog opens its fiery red eyes and kicks out its bright blue legs. Startled by the flash of colors, the predator halts. The frog uses those few precious seconds to leap to safety and climb up a nearby branch.

Tree frogs are amphibians. They can breathe on land *and* underwater. The red-eyed tree frog is one of the best-known of all tree frogs. There are more than 700 different species of this amphibian! Although tree frogs come in lots of different shapes and sizes, most share the same traits.

**Fast Fact**
*Amphibian* comes from two Greek words meaning "both lives."

▶ This red-eyed tree frog shows its surprising colors as it stretches its legs.

**Fast Fact**
A group of
frogs is called
an army.

# Frogs Everywhere

Almost all tree frogs are arboreal—they spend most of their lives in trees. These animals can live wherever there are trees and water. That's just about everywhere on the planet. But you won't find tree frogs in the driest deserts, where water is hard to find. Nor will you find them in places such as Antarctica, where it's frosty year-round. That's because tree frogs are ectothermic. Their body temperature changes based on their surroundings. When a tree frog naps in the sun, its body temperature goes up. When the frog feels too warm, it crawls under a shady leaf to lower its body temperature. Humans are different. Our body temperature stays about the same no matter what the temperature is around us.

◀ These black-eyed tree frogs live in the mountains of Guyana in South America.

# True Tree Frogs

Not all frogs that live in trees are actually "tree frogs." According to scientists, only those belonging to the Hylidae family are true tree frogs. The thing that makes them true tree frogs is a tiny bone in their toes. In tree frogs, this bone, called a phalange, is shaped like a claw. The phalange helps the frogs grip branches better.

Most tree frogs have slender bodies. A narrow shape helps them balance on thin branches. And most are small. The average tree frog is 4 inches (10.2 centimeters) long. But some are even tinier. The spring peeper is less than 1 inch (2.5 cm) long. That's half the size of a fifth grader's thumb! The largest species of tree frog is Australia's white-lipped tree frog. It can grow to over 5 in. (12.7 cm) long. The rarest tree frog is the Cinchona plantation tree frog. Only a few males and one female have been spotted in recent years.

▶ All the frogs here are true tree frogs. They come in many colors and sizes!

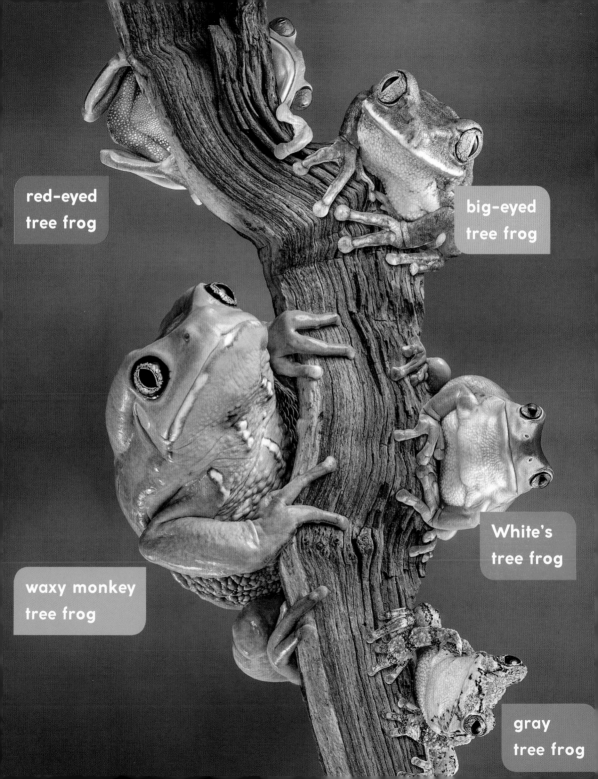

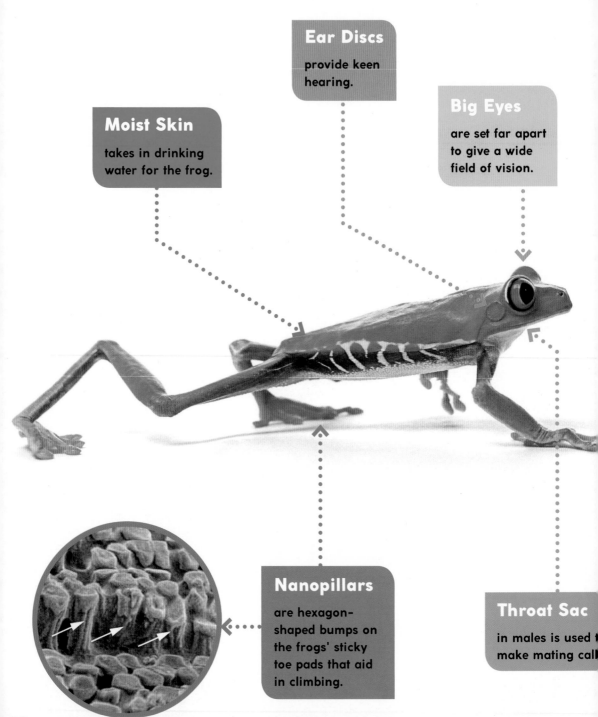

**Ear Discs**
provide keen hearing.

**Moist Skin**
takes in drinking water for the frog.

**Big Eyes**
are set far apart to give a wide field of vision.

**Nanopillars**
are hexagon-shaped bumps on the frogs' sticky toe pads that aid in climbing.

**Throat Sac**
in males is used t make mating cal

# Built for Branches

Tree frogs are perfectly built for life in the trees. Unlike frogs that live on the ground, tree frogs don't usually hop. They have long legs that they use for climbing. To go from one place to another, the frogs wrap their long toes around branches. Then they carefully pull themselves along. Tree frogs also have a special adaptation that helps them hang on to leaves: their toe pads are sticky.

Tree frogs' toe pads are made up of thousands of tiny pegs, called nanopillars. The nanopillars create a small amount of friction that keeps the frog from sliding off a slippery branch or leaf. In between the nanopillars are pores that release a watery mucus. This mucus helps the toe pads stick to especially slick surfaces. This "wet adhesion" works the way a moistened plastic suction cup clings to glass. The mucus also helps the pads self-clean when they pick up dirt!

◀ The red-eyed tree frog's eyes have vertical pupils. Some tree frogs have horizontal pupils.

**Fast Fact**
The frog's tongue is attached to the front of its mouth.

# Slime!

Tree frogs are really slimy. They have to be to survive. Tree frogs absorb water through their skin. And they breathe in two ways—through their mouths when they are on land and through their skin when they are underwater.

Tree frogs have glands that secrete, or ooze, a slimy mucus onto their skin. This mucus helps keep their skin from drying out. The mucus of some frogs, such as the gray tree frog and the Cuban tree frog, is irritating to humans. Touching one of those frogs can make many people sneeze. The waxy monkey tree frog has extra glands, located behind its eyes, that release a heavy waxy substance. The frog uses its fingers to spread the wax all over its body—like moisturizing lotion! To keep their skin moist, tree frogs also avoid dry air and direct sunlight in the daytime. They seek shady spots to rest in. When they can't avoid the sun, the frogs fold their legs underneath them so the least amount of skin is exposed.

▶ These golden palm (left) and canal zone (right) tree frogs glisten like the leaf they are sitting on.

CHAPTER 2

# Nature's Tricksters

Tree frogs are tricky. They can hide in plain sight. Some tree frogs naturally blend in with the trees they inhabit. Their colors **camouflage** them from predators. Their skin might be green like the surrounding leaves or brown and mottled like a tree trunk. Some, such as White's tree frogs, have pale skin on their bellies. To a snake or lizard looking up, the frog blends in with the sky.

Other tree frogs have the ability to change the color of their skin. For example, the gray tree frog can turn green. This change is caused by the frog's pigment. Pigment is what gives skin its color. It is affected by chemicals in the blood. Some scientists think frogs cause these pigment changes to hide themselves from danger. Others think it is caused by a difference in temperature or humidity.

A few tree frogs, such as the red-eyed tree frog, don't use camouflage for protection. Instead, they use their brilliant colors to surprise predators.

▶ It's hard to spot the gray tree frog clinging to this tree trunk.

# Looking for Bugs

Tree frogs are **carnivores**. They munch on worms and live insects, including mosquitoes, beetles, moths, flies, and sometimes hornets. The largest tree frogs can even gobble down a small lizard! All tree frogs are **nocturnal**—they hunt at night. Their bulging eyes have large **irises** that adjust to let in the most light when it's dark outside.

Sometimes tree frogs stalk their **prey**. More often they wait patiently for a tasty bug to wander by, then . . . *Zap!* The frogs unfurl their long tongues to snatch up the prey. When the frogs stick out their tongues, their saliva gets watery. As soon as an insect touches the tongue, however, the saliva turns as sticky as bubble gum.

Tree frogs generally swallow their food whole. To make swallowing a meal easier, the frogs **retract** their eyes into their skull. They use their eyes to push the prey down their throats.

◄ A tree frog's tongue measures about one-third the length of its entire body!

# Winter Is Coming

Many tree frogs live where it is warm most of the year, but some must brave cold winters. Tree frogs that live in colder areas **hibernate** in winter by burrowing under leaves or under the ground, where the temperature stays warmer. Their breathing and heart rates slow down, and they sleep for a long time. Hibernation lets the frogs save energy to survive without food in winter.

A few tree frogs, such as spring peepers, do more than hibernate. They go into a deep freeze—a kind of suspended animation. Their hearts stop pumping. Their bodies become hard. They look like they are dead. But a chemical in the frogs' bodies works like antifreeze in a car's engine. Instead of freezing solid, the animals' blood and other body fluids remain slushy, like a frozen drink. When the warm weather comes back, the fluids thaw out. The slush melts like an ice pop on a hot day.

▶ The gray tree frog can survive in subzero temperatures by freezing part of its body.

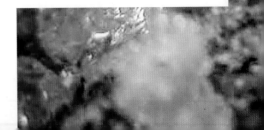

# CHAPTER 3

# Becoming Frogs

When spring arrives in the forest, the air fills with the sound of bees buzzing, birds chirping, and another noise—*Jingle, jingle! Jingle, jingle!* It sounds like sleigh bells, but it's not. It's the **mating** call of the male spring peeper tree frog. These tiny frogs are hard to see—but not to hear. They are part of a group of frogs called "chorus frogs." These frogs tend to call out at the same time. When they do, they can be heard as far away as 2 miles (3.2 kilometers).

The reason all male tree frogs make noise in spring is to attract females to mate. The males force air over their vocal cords and into inflatable pouches on their throats, called vocal sacs. Different species make different sounds. Some, like the gray tree frog, make a whistling noise. Some trill or croak. But only the Pacific tree frog makes the classic *rib-bit* sound.

▶ The inflated vocal sac lets this green tree frog "honk" for several minutes.

**Fast Fact**
Tree frog eggs
are gooey, like jelly.

# In the Clutch

Females can lay dozens, or even hundreds, of eggs at one time. A group of eggs is called a clutch. Tree frogs usually lay their eggs in water—though the body of water varies.

The Mexican bromeliad frog lays it eggs way up high in the rain forest canopy, in a tiny bit of water that has accumulated in a bromeliad. Gladiator frogs of South America make their own ponds for laying eggs. The males dig a small depression in the mud or sand near a swamp or stream that will naturally fill with water. Then they encourage females to lay the eggs in their newly constructed ponds. The red-eyed tree frog lays its eggs on leaves that hang over a pond. As the eggs hatch, the tadpoles slide into the water.

Tree frogs do not mate for life. And they don't usually wait around until the eggs hatch.

◀ These Morelet's tree frogs live in tropical rain forests. They lay their clutch of shiny eggs on leaves.

# The Tadpole Life

It usually takes about a week for frogs' eggs to hatch. But sometimes the eggs hatch early. Scientists recently discovered that the eggs of some tree frogs can sense vibration or movement when they are only four days old. Sometimes eggs that feel vibrations will hatch early to escape possible danger.

When the eggs hatch, tiny animals called tadpoles pop out. They don't look like frogs. They have large heads and long tails. They swim like fish. And like fish, they have gills. The gills pull oxygen out of the water.

Tadpoles have giant appetites. They feed on organisms that live in water, such as **algae**, kelp, and pond scum. Of course, these tiny animals are easy prey for hungry fish and birds. Many don't survive. Like all amphibians, those tadpoles that don't get eaten undergo a **metamorphosis**, a big change that will turn them into adults.

▶ **These red-eyed tree frog tadpoles don't look like frogs at all!**

# From Tadpole to Frog

Five or six weeks after the tadpoles hatch, they sprout tiny back legs. Over the next couple of weeks, their lungs begin to develop so they can breathe air. Every few days, the tadpoles push up to the surface of the water to gulp air through their mouths. Their back legs grow longer. Around three weeks later, their front legs push out.

As the tadpoles' legs are growing, their tails start to shrink. Sometimes the tadpoles crawl a little way out of the water. They check out the world from a nearby branch. Before long, their gills close up and disappear. Once this happens, the youngsters climb onto land for good. The transformation is almost complete. But the animals, now called froglets, still have stubby tails. Once the froglets' tails disappear, they will become adult frogs. About a year or more later, these frogs will look for mates. They will mate every spring for the rest of their lives— which is usually five to nine years.

◄ This Pacific tree frog tadpole is almost at the froglet stage.

# CHAPTER 4

# Meet the Frog Family

About 360 million years ago, the earliest amphibians **evolved** from fish. They looked like giant tadpoles with short legs. One of the earliest amphibians was called *Acanthostega*. It had short legs and eight toes on each foot.

Ancient amphibians spent most of their time in the water. Over time, their legs got stronger. They crawled out of the water. Soon these creatures lived mostly on land.

Frogs evolved from these ancient animals. The oldest frog skeletons ever found are over 200 million years old. **Fossils** of ancient tree frogs show they had long back legs like those of tree frogs today. But frogs that live today appeared after the dinosaurs died out about 65 million years ago.

▶ *Acanthostega* was 2 ft. (0.6 m) long and weighed 10 lb (4.5 kg).

## Flying Frog

This frog's frilly toes help it fly from branch to branch.

## Marbled Reed Frog

Members of this species start out brown and later turn bright colors.

## Starry Night Reed Frog

This frog's colors and pattern give a clue to how it got its name!

## Glass Frog

This frog lives in Mexico and Central and South America.

# Other Frogs in Trees

Even though they are not "true" tree frogs, frogs from other families also spend much of their lives in trees. These frogs have the same ancestor as tree frogs, and many have a lot in common with their tree frog cousins.

One close relative is the flying frog. Flying frogs have extra skin between their toes. They spread their toes, like a bat spreads its wings, to glide from branch to branch.

Another close cousin is the reed frog. There are many different kinds of reed frogs. They have short snouts and are often brightly colored.

A third close relative that lives in leafy habitats is the glass frog. Glass frogs have transparent skin on the underside of their bodies. You can see some of their organs through their skin—including their beating hearts!

◀ Not all frogs in trees are tree frogs, but they are related.

# A Land-Loving Cousin

Toads are related to tree frogs. However, they live mainly on land. They have short, thick legs that are suited for walking on the ground. And they have dry, bumpy skin, which reduces the loss of water through their skin. This allows animals like the red spotted toad to thrive in dry places like the Mojave Desert.

Toads can grow bigger than tree frogs. Some can be 9 in. (22.9 cm) long. To frighten predators, toads often puff up their bodies to look even bigger. And if that is not enough, they have another way to protect themselves. Many toads have glands that secrete a poison called bufotoxin. It can be deadly if eaten by small animals— and can even cause allergic reactions in some people who touch the toads.

▶ This common toad sits on a type of mushroom called a fly agaric. The cap can be up to 8 in. (20.3 cm) around.

# CHAPTER 5

# Protecting Tree Frogs

**Many tree frogs live in rain forests** and wetlands—areas that are constantly threatened by human development. As tree frog habitats shrink, their **populations** shrink, too.

The Pine Barrens tree frog in North America is already in trouble. This species faces a triple threat: loss of habitat, change in habitat, and increase in predators. People who wanted to build homes drained some swamps where these frogs lived, so the frogs lost that habitat. And building *near* other swamps lowered the acidity of the water. Pine Barrens frogs need a lot of acid in the water to survive. To make matters worse, some of their predators, such as the ribbon snake and the banded water snake, are more likely to appear when the acid levels are low.

▶ **The Pine Barrens tree frog has a distinctive side stripe.**

# Other Dangers

Water pollution is also dangerous for tree frogs. People are not always careful about keeping streams, rivers, and lakes clean. Waste and poisons in water cause trouble for everyone. But they are especially dangerous to tree frogs because these animals soak up water through their skin. Water pollution can also harm tree frogs' eggs before they hatch.

Recently, scientists have discovered a lot of sick frogs. Many frogs, including tree frogs, have been infected with a skin fungus. This fungus makes it hard for frogs to get enough water and air through their skin. Eventually, their hearts stop. Scientists are trying to figure out how to fight this disease.

Tree frogs are very cute. A lot of people buy them to keep as pets. This is also putting the population of some species at risk because of over-hunting. Wild tree frogs should not be kept as pets!

◀ The last known Rabb's fringe-limbed tree frog died in 2016.

# Tree Frog Teachers

Tree frogs aren't just cute. Scientists believe we can learn from them. Some researchers are studying tree frogs' toe pads. Understanding how these pads help frogs hold on may teach us how to make car tires that can hold on to the road better. This research may even help manufacturers improve the soles on shoes! Other scientists are looking into what makes tree frog eggs hatch early to avoid danger. They think they may learn some secrets that will apply to other animals as well. And doctors have found a substance in the skin of the White's tree frog that can be used to heal cold sores in humans.

We need to protect the tree frog population. You have already helped by learning about these amazing amphibians. You can also help them by keeping our air and water clean and our forests and wetlands healthy. That will keep tree frogs singing into the future!

▶ This scientist is testing the waxy monkey frog's skin.

# Tree Frog Family Tree

Tree frogs are amphibians. Like all amphibians, they are ectothermic and undergo a transformation called metamorphosis. They are usually born in water, where they develop lungs and other organs so they can live on land. Almost all tree frogs spend the rest of their lives in trees. This diagram shows how tree frogs are related to other amphibians. The closer together two animals are on the tree, the more similar they are.

**Frogs**
**the scientific category of "frog" includes frogs and toads**

**Salamanders**
**amphibians that keep their tails as adults and look like smooth-skinned lizards**

**Caecilians**
**amphibians that have no arms or legs and that look like large worms or silky snakes**

**Ancestor of all Amphibians**

*Note: Animal photos are not to scale.*

## Toads
frogs with bumpy
skin and short
legs for walking on
the ground

## Flying Frogs
frogs that can glide
from branch
to branch

## Poison Dart
Frogs
tiny frogs whose
bright colors warn
predators that they
are poisonous to eat

## Tree Frogs
slimy frogs that
have big eyes
and sticky toe pads
and live high in
the trees

# Words to Know

A ......... **adaptation** *(ad-ap-TAY-shun)* change a living thing goes through so it fits in better within its environment

**adhesion** *(ad-HEE-zhun)* the property of sticking very tightly to something

**algae** *(AL-jee)* small plants without roots or stems that grow mainly in water

**amphibians** *(am-FIB-ee-uhnz)* cold-blooded animals that have a backbone and that live in water and breathe with gills when young; as adults, they develop lungs and live on land

**ancestor** *(ANN-ses-tur)* a family member who lived long ago

C ......... **camouflage** *(KAM-uh-flahzh)* a way of hiding by using coloring, pattern, or shape to blend into one's surroundings

**canopy** *(KAN-uh-pee)* the upper layer of a rain forest, consisting mostly of branches, vines, and leaves

**carnivores** *(KAHR-nuh-vorz)* animals that eat meat

E ......... **ectothermic** *(ek-toe-THER-mik)* having a body temperature that varies with the temperature of the surroundings

**evolved** *(i-VAHLVD)* changed slowly and naturally over time

F ......... **fossils** *(FAH-suhls)* bones, shells, or other traces of animals or plants from millions of years ago, preserved as rock

G ......... **glands** *(GLANDZ)* organs in the body that produce or release natural chemicals

**H** ......... **habitats** *(HAB-i-tats)* the places where an animal or plant is usually found

**hibernate** *(HYE-bur-nayt)* when animals hibernate, they sleep for the entire winter; this protects them and helps them survive when the temperatures are cold and food is hard to find

**I** ......... **irises** *(EYE-risez)* the round colored parts of the eyes around the pupils

**M** ......... **mating** *(MAY-ting)* the act of pairing a male and a female in order to reproduce

**metamorphosis** *(met-uh-MOR-fuh-sis)* a complete or great change in appearance or form; a transformation

**N** ......... **nocturnal** *(nahk-TUR-nuhl)* active at night

**P** ......... **populations** *(pahp-yuh-LAY-shuhns)* all members of a species living in certain places

**predator** *(PRED-uh-tuhr)* animal that lives by hunting other animals for food

**prey** *(PRAY)* an animal that is hunted by another animal for food

**R** ......... **retract** *(ruh-TRAKT)* to draw back in

**S** ......... **secrete** *(si-KREET)* to produce and release a liquid

**snouts** *(SNOUTS)* the long fronts part of animals' heads, which include the nose, mouth, and jaws

**species** *(SPEE-sheez)* one of the groups into which animals and plants are divided; members of the same species can mate and have offspring

**V** ......... **vibrations** *(vye-BRAY-shuhnz)* the feelings or sensations of something moving back and forth rapidly

# Find Out More

**BOOKS**

- Gilpin, Daniel. *Tree Frogs, Mud Puppies & Other Amphibians*. Minneapolis, MN: Compass Point Books, 2006.

- Lunis, Natalie. *Tricky Tree Frogs* (Amphibiana). New York: Bearport Publishing, 2010.

- Robbins, Lynette. *Tree Frogs* (Jump!). New York: PowerKids Press, 2012.

- Wechsler, Doug. *Treefrogs*. New York: PowerKids Press, 2002.

- Weir, Diana Loiewski. *Tree Frogs*. Mankato, MN: Creative Company, 2000.

To find more books and resources about animals, visit:
## scholastic.com

# Index

# Index (continued)

# About the Author

Moira Rose Donohue is the author of more than 25
children's books, most of them nonfiction. She loves
animals of all kinds, but especially her dog, Petunia.
She and Petunia live in St. Petersburg, Florida.
www.moirarosedonohue.net